STINGRAY FOR A DAY

STINGRAY FOR A DAY
Copyright 2021 by Chris Rohaley, Chris 51
All story, art, and layout by Chris 51
All right reserved. No part of this book may be reproduced or transmitted in any form or by any means, electronic or mechanical, including photocopying, recording, or by any information storage and retrieval system, without written permission of the publisher.
ISBN 978-0-578-97944-1
ALPHA GEEK PUBLISHING
3585 Main St.
Springfield, OR 97478
CHRIS 51
email-Chris@chris51.com

For
Ryker

I told my son this story on a cold morning walk in the spring of 2021. He said, "Daddy, you need to tell that story. It sounds like a Disney football movie or something I would love to read or watch." I began writing it later that day . . .

FORWARD

If Chris 51's journey in football doesn't motivate you then you've never given your all to the game. Chris definitely gave everything he had to the sport. His story will inspire you and make you question your own drive and dedication towards a dream. Anyone could take a lesson on having true heart and grit from Chris 51 and benefit from his real underdog tale on never giving up no matter the odds stacked against you. It's a collection of attributes needed to succeed in both football and life.

Stingray For A Day reminded me of some of the trials, hardships and rewards from my own journey to the pinnacle level of football. It rekindled memories that branded the love for this game in me that still burns bright. -*Akili Smith*

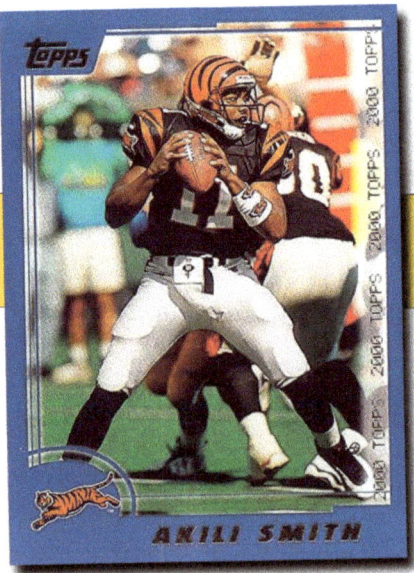

After a stellar career at the University of Oregon Akili Smith was the 3rd overall pick by the Bengals in the first round of the 1999 NFL draft. He later played in NFL Europe and the Canadian Football League. The multi-talented Smith was also drafted by the Pittsburgh Pirates and played minor league baseball before his football career.

A Completely True Story...

PREFACE

This is not a brag rag about fame and grandeur. It's definitely not a story about accolades or stature. It is a tale that defines the spirit of sacrifice, dedication, and passion. It exemplifies the meaning of having heart and grit. This is a motivational sports story--but not one that you may be accustomed to.

I didn't come from nothing and turn into a Hall of Famer or sports icon. I wasn't abused or orphaned, and I didn't grow up in poverty. I fought age, lack of talent, doubters--and myself--to chase a dream I thought was long lost. I manifested my own destiny, worked my-ass off, and defied the odds stacked against me to become a semi-pro football rookie at the age of 30.

I didn't do it for the money, because there wasn't any. I didn't do it to be noticed by scouts or start a new career. I didn't do it to get girls; in fact, I almost lost my girl in doing so. I did it because I felt a void and unfulfilled in a game I loved above all others. I did it to prove to myself that I could.

There were no endorsements and no retirement packages; hell, there wasn't even insurance to cover injuries. There were no trading cards made or names read over loudspeakers.

This was a nothing team that went nowhere in a nothing league full of undrafted college kids looking for another opportunity or NFL camp rejects who got busted or released. It has long since been forgotten, faded by the sun of Florida sports oblivion, at least for those who watched in the stands.

None of that mattered to me. To me it was still a class of professional football. It was the best of the best that were left or forgotten. It was a second chance at my first love.

THE EPIC PEE 1

I whipped into the parking lot of Stevie Tomatoes Sports Bar like a bat out of hell. I don't think I've ever had to piss so bad in my whole life. My eyeballs were floating in urine at this point. I had one hand clutching my crotch and the other on the wheel. I almost sideswiped a Beamer as I chose my parking spot, and at that point I didn't really care.

Even though the desire to fill my empty stomach with some delicious, sexy, hot buffalo wings was severe, it failed in comparison to emptying my bladder.

I stepped to the urinal and unloaded my little chub to a chorus of a thousand little cherubs singing a relief tone of "ahhhhhhhh" in my mind. Sweet relief. I was returning to my senses. The gods were shining on me that day. Any man will tell you that there are few feelings in this world better than draining the lizard when it's full to the tip.

At first, I was thanking Jesus for allowing me to make it to the porcelain God in time so I didn't have to eat my sexy buffalo wing lunch in piss-soaked Carhartts. But it turns out that wasn't why I was meant to be at that exact urinal at that exact time in this exact restaurant in Ft. Myers, Florida, on a hot, sunny afternoon.

My mind was slowly returning to awareness, while my bladder was unloading faster than a Deion Sanders 40-yard dash, when a poor excuse for an advertisement came into focus in front of my eyes. It was a crappy black and white photocopy poorly hung on the wall, clinging on for dear life by a lonely piece of tape that looked like it had been stuck on by someone who'd just eaten a greasy pile of those sexy buffalo wings.

Was I reading this correctly? "Do you want to play semi-pro football? Do you want to relive your football dreams or get noticed by scouts?" My answer was hell yes to the first, and I don't give a shit to the second.

I moved in for a closer look, wiener still in hand shrinking into oblivion with just a few remaining drips reminding me he was still there. At this point I didn't give a crap about that little dick anymore. I was reading about football--more importantly, playing football.

Few things come between a man and his cock. Football, a woman, and . . . well, that's about it, and in that exact order of importance. Any true football fan will understand this, and if you don't, well, then just stop reading now because you don't deserve this inspirational and erotic story about the love of balls--footballs!

I continued to read the flyer. "Tryouts." Wait, what? "Tryout to be part of the Florida Stingrays semi-pro football team." Now you have my attention, you dirty little flyer. "Tryouts August 1st at Cypress Lake High School. Contact Head Coach John Torregrossa to register now."

That would give me two months to get in tip-top shape. Should I do this? Could I do this? I'm strong and tough, but I am also slow and short (in football standards). I am fucking resilient, though, and I have more heart and passion than anyone I know. That is what drives me in life. But I am 29 years old and would be 30 at the time of minicamp. That is old as hell. In football years that's like 80.

What began as a typical day digging ditches for sewer lines in the hot-ass Florida sun for my dad's plumbing company took a sudden and exotic turn.

Little did I know that I was coming to a decision that would forever change my life.

THE UN-EPIC PEEWEE 2

My youth football career was nothing short of, well, nothing. In the late 1970s-early 1980s there was no Pee Wee tackle football in Oregon. In fact, there was no football of any kind until 4th grade. Then you had to play flag for a couple of years before finally getting to strap on shoulder pads in middle school.

In 1983 I was poised to be a flag football superstar. I had collected more trading cards than any of my friends, and I could name almost every starting player on every NFL team. I had all the gumball machine mini-helmets, still in mint condition and every sticker album produced. I knew football! The only problem was, I didn't know how to play yet. Furthermore, my little twig-like body wasn't as big as the other kids'.

Washington Elementary School football Coach Tom Winbigler, a former college Hall of Fame player, barely noticed me. I'm not sure if he ever even knew my name. I was unassuming and forgettable at that stage in athletics.

19 · Trader · 83

Aside from skateboarding and karate, I pretty much stunk at sports. I was small, weak, slow, unaggressive, timid, and pretty much everything a head coach doesn't want in a player. I was the kid whose only importance was an added body to fill out a roster to allow a team to exist.

I was put at the position where I assume

the coach thought I could do the least harm to the team: defensive end. With our fast outside linebackers and corners, they could pick up the flags that got passed me, which were a lot.

I did nothing memorable.

19 · Trader · 85

Fifth grade *(photo bottom opposite page)* was more of the same. I was smaller and slower than my teammates, got less playing time, and made even less of an impact. Even if I were given the same opportunities, I'm not sure that I would have made the most of them at that point in my life. I loved the game with all my passion, but it did not love me back.

I did nothing memorable.

Sixth grade arrived and so did helmets. We finally got into the pads that we were so jealous of watching older friends and siblings wearing in the past few years.

We got to hit! The only problem was we got hit back. I wasn't really a fan of that. I gravitated toward defense because I would've rather lay the hit on someone than receive it. I was still too small and too slow. In fact, I had to skateboard to the local vitamin store to buy weight-gainer shakes just to make the 86-pound weight limit to be qualified to play. I only made the weight restrictions because I soaked

my shoes in water so they would weigh more. The rest of middle school was more of the same. I was stuck at defensive end where there is little glory. We were never allowed to blitz in and get a quarterback sack. Our job was to contain so no running back sweeps or reverses got around us.

It was boring and often uneventful. All I wanted was to get a sack.

I wanted to be a linebacker. They got all the glory and all the sacks. The middle linebacker was the defensive captain and the quarterback of the offense. Linebackers were studs, the cool kids, if there is such a thing on the defensive side of the ball. I wished that I could demand that kind of respect among my peers. Unfortunately, it just wasn't me at that point in my life. I was not a leader. I wasn't even a follower. I was just kind of stuck somewhere in the quiet middle. I was oblivious to the oblivion.

I was tossed in at full back a couple times when we had a good lead, but it was typically to block for the faster half backs. I think I got four carries my entire middle school career, and about seven total yards, which was still better than my ZERO sacks on defense!

I do remember getting a hand off on a dive up the middle one time when we were on the five-yard line. I saw an open hole and my one chance at glory. I was actually going to score a touchdown. I'd never dreamed this would happen. I kept running, one yard down, four to go. Two yards, then three. Then it happened. I was just one giant leap from the end zone and a defender pushed my teammate down right in front of me. I didn't see him quickly enough and tripped right over him, landing a foot away from the fame and glory of a touchdown. I fell over my own teammate and ruined my one chance to score like all my friends already had.

My only middle school football memory was that failure. Coming so close to a meaningless throwaway touchdown may not have been a big deal to the average player, but it was huge to below

-average me.

I wasn't aware enough to take away any life lessons from my middle school time on the field; all I did was dream of different times on different fields. Instead of working harder and sacrificing Atari time, I just told myself I would do better the next year, without doing anything to actually make myself better.

TRAINING DAY 3

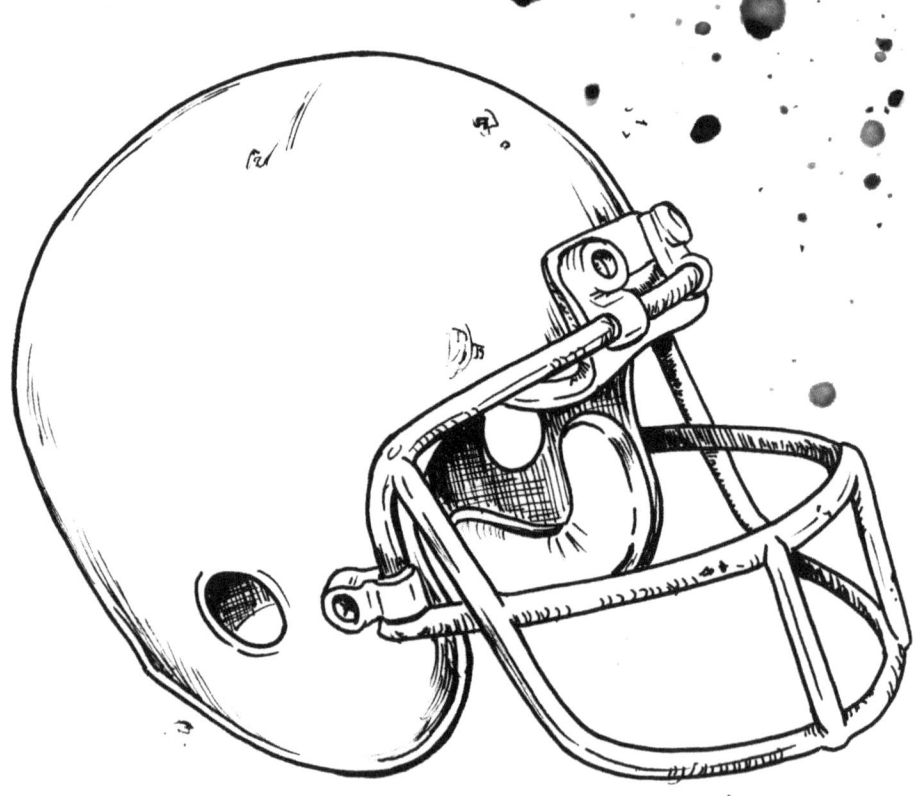

Like I said, in football years, 29 is old, and 30 is almost ancient. It's like being 80 in normal years. Bodies start breaking down and injuries are far more frequent and severe. Twenty-nine is when players are retiring or winding down their long careers, not beginning.

Logically, it was a horrible age for me to begin a professional football career and an age that very few have ever attempted it, if any. All the odds were stacked against me. Did that deter me? Hell no! Like Han said to C-3PO in Star Wars: "never tell me the odds."

Was I even in shape? Well, I did lift weights regularly and had at least 3-4 times per week religiously since high school. I wasn't a bodybuilder by any means, but I was tight in all the right places aside from a little gut from too many cookie rituals before bedtime. But was I in football shape? Hell no!

I jogged a couple times per week, maybe a couple miles, and I hated every step more than the last. It had been a decade since I'd done any kind of sprints or serious work on a field. I wasn't rusty--I was rusted.

My body was going to need to be transformed. I was a bumblebee, and I needed to become Optimus Prime. My mind would also need to be right. I would need to have total focus and dedication. If I was going to do this and realize my dream of playing football at a higher level and accomplishing something on the field of battle that I'd always felt was missing from my life, then I would have to follow my heart until the end.

I had nothing to prove to anyone other than myself. This wasn't to prove anyone wrong. Nobody outside my immediate family even knew that I was attempting it, and they knew that nothing they could have said would've stopped me anyway. No, I had no motivation other than my own need and desire to fulfill my football goals from long ago.

After my senior-year injury (which will be further discussed later), something more than just a broken hand was left on that field. Something that only a passionate man and true fan of the game can understand. I loved the sport like a brother or mother; it was somehow ingrained in my DNA and a part of my soul. I never had the chance to really prove myself or leave it all out there on the field, and not to anyone other than myself. I never got that special memory that would last me a lifetime. I never got glory. I never got redemption for that most important year of my athletic career that was lost. I was unfulfilled, and it gnawed at me every time I watched a game on TV or played catch in the street with a buddy. I was not a football player--just a fan--and that wasn't enough for me to live with. I needed something more, and this was my chance.

It didn't take long to convince my mind of something that it already knew needed to happen. The seeds of desire and motivation were already there, they just needed a little water and room to grow. I was about to give them a tidal-wave force of stimulation.

There are two types of men in this world: those who make excuses and those who manifest their own destiny. There are those who succumb to pressure and accept failure, and there are those who will let absolutely nothing or nobody get in their way, no matter the cost. There is something incredible and magical that can happen in very select individuals when they realize a dream is within grasp.

There are men who give a little effort and allow that dream to pass them by because they simply cannot give or aren't willing to give that extra part of their life and soul and time to capture it.

Then there are men who are so driven by their dream that there is no amount of pain or loss that will stop them until they reach the end and accomplish their goal. They can't sleep or slow down until it's done, even if it kills them or causes irreparable damage along the way. Men who are willing to make that sacrifice are the champions of their own fate, and they can rest happily and satisfied when it's all over.

I was that second kind of man. I just didn't realize it yet, but it was in me. My dad was that way. I never realized that until after he was gone. But when you grow up seeing dedication, sacrifice, and drive as part of your normal daily routine, it becomes second nature. I am so thankful that I had those daily life lessons, and they shaped who I was and who I would later become in life.

My mind was right. Luckily for me, that was the easy part. For most, that is what will break a man the fastest. In my own mind I was already a professional football player; I just needed to peel back the laced-up leather layers to reveal it.

My mind was set. Now it was time for my body to get right. It needed to match my mental shape. It had some work to do and do quickly.

I had exactly two months to turn this 29-year-old plumber's body into a football body. I wasn't going to half-ass this. I never half-assed anything in life. I was raised better than that. I was about to push my body to the extreme, to levels of exertion that I never had before, or that I even knew were available in me.

I had one chance, just one chance, for football redemption. The football gods revealed themselves and I saw their light. I had to give it everything I had; I couldn't waste a moment of this opportunity. I wasn't going to let myself down ever again. This was going to be the hardest, and hopefully most rewarding, thing that I had ever attempted.

Bring it on.

4 TABBIES

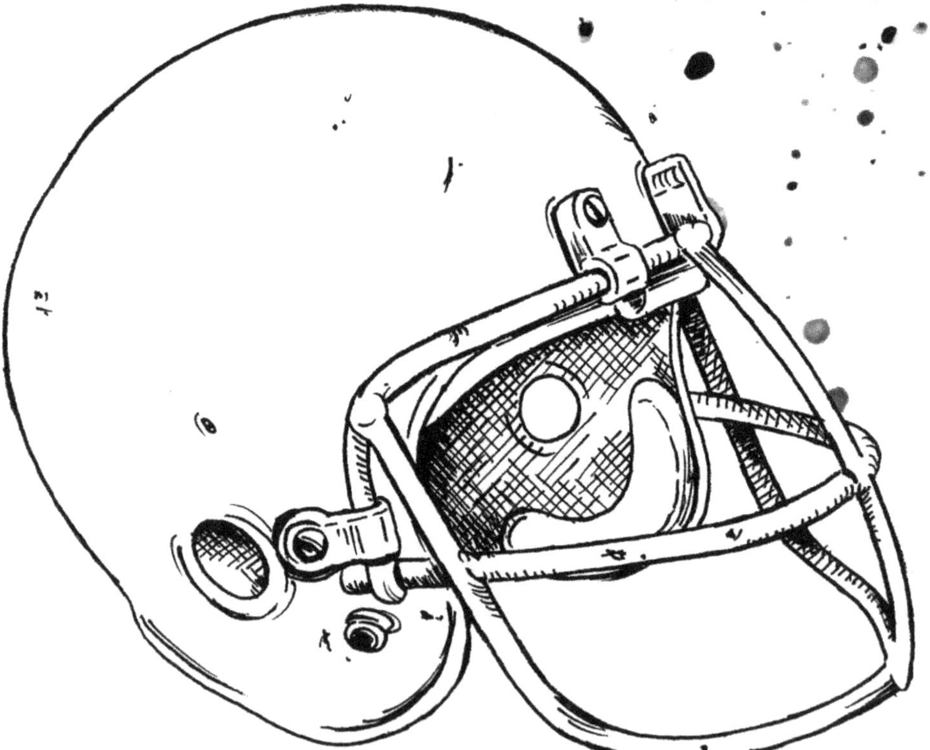

Along came high school and the chance for redemption and to prove myself, not only to coaches, but to myself. New coaches and a new school meant new opportunities, and I was ready.

But my body still wasn't. In 1988 I was still puny and slow. I was still fearful and timid.

Sheldon High School in Eugene, Oregon, is now considered a local powerhouse school. They are always top in the league, often winning State. In 1988 they were just showing signs of that greatness and shedding the cloak of cellar dweller.

However, as a freshman about to join the ranks of high school football prowess, I wasn't worried about my performance on the field yet. I wasn't worried about coaches noticing me or potential injury. Nope! I was worried about only one thing. It was the same thing all my best friends were worried about: tabbies!

What the hell are "tabbies" you ask? Well, we were asking the same thing during the summer of 1988. We had been hearing about tabbies all summer and the rumors and horrors surrounding them.

Tabbies were the initiation into high school football. It was unspoken to adults, but the upcoming freshmen knew all too well about them.

Tabbies were just salt tablets. But it's what you were made to do with them that scared us all.

Our locker room showers were one long, wide room of solid pale green and white old tile that stretched on for what seemed like at least 50 feet. The upperclassmen would turn on all the showers to the hottest setting possible, creating a scalding hot alley of flesh-burning death. Freshmen would have to get on their hands and knees at one end of the room, buck naked. Tablets were placed on the floor in front of their faces, and they were told to go! The kids would have to get down and push the salt tablets with only their noses while crawling across the tile. As they nosed the tablets down the lava-like floor, they were whipped with wet towels on their bare asses. They were cheered and belittled as they had to push that little tablet all the way to the other end of the room before it melted. As you can imagine, the hot water melted the salt quickly, so hustle was essential. Mild burns and sore knees were the least of your worries. It was the ridicule of dick size or fat rolls that scared everyone the most.

After summertime daily doubles were over, school started, and regular after-school practice began. Tabbies weren't instituted until regular season practice began. I'm not sure if it was to weed out all the kids who quit after the torture of daily doubles to go play soccer, or simply to have two more weeks to scare the incoming freshmen.

I'd never had much luck up to that point in my childhood. I was never lucky on the field, on the diamond, on the court, or even with the girls. So, when I say that I needed a lucky break, I was due.

The lucky break for me, and all my freshmen teammates, came just in time. It was the day before tabbies, and the nightmares were hitting stronger than a Lawrence Taylor sack on Joe Theismann.

The coaches got together for a meeting and decided that tabbies were no longer a constructive team-building exercise. I think it might have been more about the complaints. Maybe there was pressure from a scared kid ratting tabbies out to a parent. Whatever it was, tabbies were officially over by order of the big boss man himself, the head coach.

Needless to say, the upperclassmen who'd had to go through the torture of tabbies themselves were not happy. In fact, they were downright pissed, and took it out on us "spoiled" kids on the field. We felt their retribution for days.

In today's society, the tabbies initiation would get the entire staff fired and probably land some kids in juvie and make national headlines. Although I was scared shitless and so grateful the long-standing tradition stopped at our year, I can see why they began and what they meant to the camaraderie of the team. Before they got out of hand, they did, in a weird and twisted way, bring teammates closer and bonded them through mutually assured torture. It united the team and made the freshmen feel accepted in a situation where they were scared just being new to high school. If you could make it through tabbies, the rest of high school would be a breeze, and you could make it through any challenge.

TRAINING HARD 5

I worked my ass to the damn bone for 10 hours a day.

My boss was my dad, and he didn't take shit! He made me earn my money. I don't know if it was to teach me important lessons about work ethic or if he was just simply a dickhead, but nonetheless it happened daily. I definitely learned the value of hard earning.

I laid sewer pipe. Not only did I lay pipe in deep ditches, I had to first dig those ditches by hand. Not only did I have to dig ditches all-day long, I also had to do it in the sweltering Florida heat and humidity. It was enough to kill a man, and if I were to attempt it today, it certainly would.

My father was not sympathetic to my desire to try out for a pro football team; in fact, he thought it was a fool's errand. Not to mention it would take my focus away from my work and time away from his company. My desires gnawed at his soul nearly as much as they did at my own.

I assured him that I would train after work hours and on weekends, and when practice started it would be in the evenings after work. He still didn't approve, and I'm not sure he even understood because he wasn't a big jock in high school. He was more the muscle-car stoner type. But he was a huge Miami Dolphins fan, as was my entire family in Florida, so I have a feeling that deep down he was rooting for me.

So, my normal day was as follows: Wake up at 6:00 a.m. for work. Dig ditches and lay pipe in the 100+ degree Florida July and August days for 10 hours. Get home completely exhausted and scrape my ass off the floor to go on a jog. Come home from several torturous miles in the prime heat of the day and run straight into the hot garage to lift weights. Eat plain chicken breasts, white rice, and broccoli with a gallon of water for dinner, then study football books and videos. Finally, try to sleep but stay up all night thinking about what more or what else I could do to prepare.

The next day was more of the same except I traded the weights for going to the local high school, Cypress Lake, to run up and down bleachers and do sprints.

This routine continued every single day, no exception, no breaks, no excuses.

I was physically exhausted and pushing my body to the brink. I was constantly on the cusp of pain, but not enough to slow me down for one second. A little pain helped motivate me to get stronger and overcome that weakness.

Mentally, I was a beast. Nothing stood in my way and nothing discouraged my resolve. Not even my wife, who was getting very annoyed at this point.

Oddly enough, I didn't even care. We had been married a few years and the spark was already smoldering. She didn't understand my passion, and she felt little of her own for much of anything, so how could she? She didn't like football and that was already a problem itself. I certainly wasn't going to let her stand in the way of my dreams or derail my train of focus.

I admit, I was a selfish asshole, and she didn't deserve it. She was a kind person. But it's hard to get behind something that you cannot comprehend. If you don't feel any deep-rooted passion, how can you support it? My football dream didn't end our marriage (that took care of itself later), but it certainly didn't help it.

Back to the training. It consumed me. It took over and became my identity. Every spare minute was dedicated to getting ready for football camp.

I grabbed a friend on the weekends to throw me passes so I could work on routes. I had it in my head that I was going to follow in my idol's footsteps and become the next Steve Largent, even if it was only for one season. I was slow and built nothing like a receiver, but that didn't stop me from training like one. I ran hundreds of routes, more than I ever did in high school. Wait, I never ran them in high school. That's right; I wanted to be a receiver but never got the chance due to missing my senior year. So, I was basically learning a new position that I'd never played in my life and expecting to make a semi-professional football team in doing so. I also hadn't played a down of football in well over a decade. But I was going to make the team regardless. Yep, that was my thought process, and nobody could convince me otherwise.

I watched hundreds of videos, mostly from the master route-maker Steve Largent, and taught myself. I had played defense my entire life, but I wanted to try and emulate my hero. He was the whole reason I was here and the true reason behind my love of the game.

Steve Largent either led the league or was among the league-leaders in receiving stats every year. He was a perennial All-Pro. He was smaller and slower than all his peers, but he never let his physical stature slow him down. Largent played with class and style and was a true professional; never getting in trouble on or off the field. He was the ultimate role model. I was proud to call him my hero.

Since I was a child, I'd related to Largent. I was a kid version of him. I was too slow and too small and had the bark of an underdog my entire youth. He was the average man's man. He did what we all wanted to do, and with little God-given talent, he did it all with heart and sheer will. Largent gave hope to me and all the average kids. Maybe, just maybe, if he could do it, then I could do it. Sure, my quest was nowhere near the magnitude of his accomplishments, but to me it was just as important. I wasn't doing this to set all the Largent-type records. I just wanted to prove to myself that I could do it, and do it against all odds of age, size, and experience.

I was going to make it and I was going to wear #80 as tribute to my lifelong hero.

My high school career was not a career at all. It was a four-year stint interrupted by relocation, injury, and fear.

We already know that my freshman year began under a dark cloud of fear and intimidation of initiation. After the torture of tabbies culture, I was then introduced to my first real peer-pressure initiation. Just a few days into regular season practice I got into my first fight, and with one of my best friends in the world.

I was hanging out with a new kid who had moved to town for a portion of the summer. I'm not sure if it was jealousy or just bullying, but somehow, he'd started spreading rumors that I was better at football than my friend Jeff "The Kid" DeRieux. Now, to say that either of us was better than the other was like picking the two runts of any blind litter and watching them find their ways to the last deformed, non-functioning, old, shriveled-up tit. We were the two smallest kids on the team, and probably two of the least aggressive.

The Kid and I had been best friends since we'd met in the same neighborhood when we were six years old. For some reason, this new boy didn't like that or me hanging out with The Kid, and he pitted us against each other. The rumors spread through practice faster than a Ray Lewis blitz, and before I knew it, our peers had set up a fight for us after the conclusion of practice. Neither of us wanted to be there or make fists at each other, but the peer pressure was so thick we couldn't see clearly through it. It was either fight or be labeled as pussies forever and lose any shred of dignity and respect we had, which wasn't much to begin with.

We got shoved into each other to start it and some wild haymakers were thrown. It quickly ended with name calling, mostly from the crowd, and we each went home upset.

What nobody knows is that I cried the entire skateboard ride home. I'd just fought my best friend and it killed me on the inside. Even though neither of us was really to blame, I was ashamed I'd let it happen, as was he. I'd experienced my first fist fight, and it left more of a scar on my heart than any punch could on my body.

We made up days later, and I vowed to myself at that young age to never let anyone peer-pressure me, control me, or bully me around ever again, and I haven't!

That was the beginning of my high school football career, and this was all in the first couple weeks of practice. Things did not get much better from there.

I showed absolutely zero potential on the field. Other kids ran faster, hit harder, and even had more heart. I was lost. I was playing because I loved the game, but my love of the game didn't propel me to do great things yet. I didn't understand sacrifice and the art of pushing myself to the limits. I think I just enjoyed playing with my friends more than anything. That was my driving force as a freshman.

Game time was no different. My ass was in great shape from riding the bench so hard. I got into my old, typical, token defensive end spot each game where I could do the least amount of damage. I got a tackle here and there, but most of the time I was the last one jumping on the pile of the faster and stronger kids. I didn't have one single moment of glory to speak of: not a single interception or fumble recovery and no touchdowns. All I really wanted was a sack. I'd been a defensive player my whole life, so even though everyone dreams of a touchdown, I didn't really think it was a possibility--more of a miracle if it happened. Playing on the D-line, especially at the end of it, you just dream of a sack. At my age and level, you weren't allowed to rush in, only run straight and contain the edge against sweeps and reverses. So unless the QB rolled out your direction, it wasn't going to happen unless you broke the rules and wanted to get the wrath of the coach and be benched even more.

My sophomore year was even worse. Well, actually, nonexistent. My family was planning a move back to Florida where I was born, and they sent me ahead for the summer to live with my aunt and get my first summer job working for her law office. I was excited to do it but missed my friends immediately.

I began my sophomore year at Port St. Lucie High and was lost from the start. I was a loner and couldn't make any friends. I didn't know how. I'd never had to make new friends; I was used to having the same two best friends my entire life. I ate lunch alone in the courtyard. I was too shy to talk to girls and years away from finding my confidence or pit-bull mentality. I was a lost puppy.

I knew nothing about the football program and didn't even know whom to approach. I was scared to ask the other boys around the school who appeared to be jocks. Maybe I feared rejection or maybe it was fear of getting in another fight that so drastically scarred me the year before. Whatever it was, I was a little pussy and I regret not stepping up and being more, doing more, and becoming more! My parents weren't around to push me, and my dad was too busy with work back in Oregon to notice what was going on in my life. I never told anyone about what I was going through. I hated that school. I hated my life, and I despised who I had become. I was stuck in a pit that I couldn't climb out of. I needed help but was too timid to ask for it.

Before I knew it, my cowardliness caused me to miss the football season. That was the one thing I'd really wanted to do, and probably the one thing that could have saved me. It is easy to make friends on the field; you share too much mutual pain not to. Anyone who says sports are a waste of time is absolutely wrong. Sports create bonds of teammates that bind through both winning and losing together, which translate to friendships that can last a lifetime.

Fortunately, my dad got new work and the family decided to stay in Oregon until my little brother graduated high school, so they sent for me to return home halfway through the school year. I was reunited with my lifelong friends. My football season was lost but my friendships were found.

My junior year was an improvement, but I still didn't leave my mark because I didn't yet understand how to leave it all on the field.

I was still one of the smaller kids and had less athletic talent than pretty much most of the team. To say I was average would be a nice compliment, but probably stretching the kindness a little too far.

I did see more playing time--on JV, of course. I'm not sure if it was because we just had a player shortage or the superstar kids who played two-ways needed more rest so they could focus more on offensive-skilled positions. Either way, I was the lucky beneficiary and able to start more at defensive end. I got a few more tackles and felt a little more comfortable in my own shoes. I still didn't have that aggressive fire that most of my teammates naturally had, but I was beginning to feel a little spark inside.

Last game of the season we were playing in Marshfield High School. It had rained the night before, so like their namesake, the field was a muddy marsh. The perfect condition for a high school JV game. Those are the field conditions you dream of, the slick terrain that takes you back to sliding in the mud on your neighborhood park field as a kid with your friends. The kind that pisses mom off because she knows that clothes washing is going to be a nightmare and she's going to have to spray you off with the hose outside in the freezing cold before you're allowed to sprint through the house and jump into the shower.

The game was almost over, and the starting middle linebacker got hurt. I was on the wet bench, of course, and got the call to get my ass in there. Wait, what? Middle linebacker? That was the big dog spot. That was the captain of the D. The main man. I had never played there before; I didn't even know what the hell to do.

I ran up to the coach in a frenzy. "Coach, I've never played that position, what do I do?"

In his infinite wisdom he grabbed my facemask, looked into my eyes and said, "Tackle anything that comes up the middle at you. If I call a blitz, go sack the quarterback." I heard the magical word "sack," and that was all I needed. That spark that I'd briefly felt at moments during the season just ignited into a fierce fire. I had never felt any rush like that. That feeling is what it was all about. I finally got it. In that instant, I truly understood football.

We broke the defensive huddle and I looked to my right and left to make sure I was in line with the outside linebackers. I think I was in position. I was too excited to be nervous and too nervous to be scared.

The opposing QB looked right into my eyes while he was calling out his cadence. Why did he do that? Holy shit, the play was coming to me, I just knew it. I then redirected my focus to the running back behind him, and he was looking right at me. Now I really knew without a doubt. The center snapped the ball and the quarterback turned to the left to hand off to the running back. I saw a giant hole open up that the lineman created for the back to burst through. That left me as the only line of defense. I bolted for the hole; this opportunity wasn't going to pass me by. I collided with the tailback a millisecond after he received the handoff. I bulldozed through him and tackled him for a loss of several yards, behind the original line of scrimmage. I jumped up excited and my teammates all patted me on the butt and gave me high fives.

I had never had that kind of opportunity and I made the most of it. My first play at linebacker and I nailed it. Wow! I loved this damn position! I was pumped up; my fire was in a roar. It was the single best play of my entire football career up to that point. I finally had a positive memory. It was a routine good play for anyone else, but for me it was huge.

I lined back up for the next play, adrenaline still pumping through my chest. Seconds later the ball snapped. I saw the running back drift out to the flat and the tight end going out for a pass, so football logic told me to drop back in pass coverage. I knew the game. I knew what my responsibility should be. The QB released a short pass, and the trajectory was too low. One of our defensive linemen got his big paw up and swatted at it. It tipped in such a way that sent it flipping end over end in my direction. I dove for the ball and was inches from intercepting it before it hit the ground. Damn, my second play at linebacker, and I'd suddenly amassed a tackle-for-loss and near interception already. This was the greatest game of my life in just two plays.

Time was nearly out, and Marshfield had enough ticks left for one last play. They were behind by a bit, so their only hope was to complete a Hail Mary and hope for an onside kick. That meant pass. That also meant a blitz for me.

The ball was snapped and had just barely reached the quarterback's hands before I was already through the offensive line. I dove for his waist as he received the snap and tackled him where he stood flat-footed.

Holy shit, I just got my sack!

It was what I had dreamed of doing my whole career, and it was everything I could have imagined and more. It was meaningless in the outcome of the game since we had basically already won, and I didn't even know if half the team noticed it. But I did, and that's what mattered to me.

In three plays I had tackled the running back in the backfield for a loss, a near interception, and a sack! It was the culmination of my career goals in about a two-minute span. Then the game whistle blew, and it was all over, the season ended.

Little did I know, my high school career was about to end.

My senior year began with high hopes. Coming off my memorable last game from the previous season, I had a newfound outlook on the sport and within myself. There was something a little different about me. I felt a touch of confidence. Not a lot, but enough to try hitting a little harder and pushing myself a little further. It was a glimpse of the man I would become.

You bet your ass that that season I was trying out for linebacker. I also wanted to be a backup receiver. I wanted to just catch a pass or two and emulate Steve Largent. I set my goals high, probably too high, but why not aim for the stars because I would have still been satisfied with landing somewhere in the space below.

But a week into practice the unthinkable happened. The ridiculous and embarrassing happened. I was trying to snap my chin strap on my old-ass helmet while standing in line for receiver pass route drills. This helmet was probably leftover from the 1970s, and just a concussion away from being thrown in the trash. But back then, there were no equipment protocols like there are now, so whoever got in line the fastest at gear handout got the 10-year-old equipment, and if you were late or not paying attention you were stuck with the leftover 20-year-old shit.

The chin strap would not snap. It was almost my turn in line and the damn thing was rusted or oxidized. I didn't want my helmet shifting on my face and to miss seeing the ball while I was trying to impress coaches and earn that backup receiver spot. I gave it one last big push with my thumb and I heard a snap. Unfortunately, it wasn't the chin strap--it was my thumb. Yes, I dislocated it trying to get my stupid, old chin strap buckled.

I had to play it tough. I wanted to scream in agony, but my need to preserve my dignity and manhood outweighed everything at this point. I sucked it up and ran the route. Luckily for me it was a shitty pass and in an instant, I thought that if I attempted to dive for the ball, I could fall awkward on my hand and pretend that was how I hurt my thumb. That is precisely what I did, and I pulled it off masterfully. I hopped up clinching my hand and wincing in pain. The coach examined my hand and sent me into the trainer's office.

The trainer popped my thumb back into place and wrapped it up. He told me I could still run my routes but to tell the coaches to just not throw the ball because he didn't want me to catch it and pop my thumb back out of the socket. He sent me back out to the field with little sympathy and my manliness still intact.

I gave the coach the trainer's message and he said no problem, hop back in line. My turn had arrived, and I ran a short fly route as fast as I could. Like a dumbass, the coach fired the ball at me anyway. Since I wasn't expecting a throw, I was late to react. Your instinct is to put your hands up to catch the pass. In the process of doing so, I suddenly remembered that my right thumb was taped up and extended out like a target. But it was too late. It all happened in a flash. I awkwardly flung my left hand out to deflect the ball so it wouldn't hit my already injured thumb. In doing so, my left thumb caught the tip of the ball and the force bent my thumb back 90 degrees the wrong way. I heard a pop and felt my thumb touch the back side of my wrist. The ball was more like a missile firing in toward me, and my thumb joint exploded.

I was done. I knew it instantly.

I went straight to the emergency room. My thumb was totally messed up, and the doctor informed me that not only was I out for the season, but I was probably out for all sports my senior year. No baseball, no wrestling. He put a Sheldon Irish green-colored cast on my hand that went all the way up to my mid-forearm. I was stricken with pain, but not in my thumb. My heart was crushed.

I left the hospital with two injured thumbs. I was humiliated and defeated. I immediately ripped the tape off my sprained thumb when I got home. There was no way I was going to school the next day with two busted thumbs for my peers to make fun of. Fuck that!

That motherfuckin coach hadn't listened to me, hadn't paid attention, or just hadn't cared, and he ruined my senior year. He'd deprived me of my final season of tackle football. The year you look forward to from the time you first strap on shoulder pads. No glory. No playing home games at the illustrious Autzen Stadium, home of the Oregon Ducks, and every young boy's dream field to play on while growing up in this area.

I had finally felt like I'd found a spot on a football team where I could contribute and maybe even shine once in a while. I had no delusions of grandeur and knew I wasn't going to play college ball, but I'd finally found the passion, and then it was ripped away from me in an instant. My football career was finished.

I never got to play one down of varsity football. I was stuck sitting in the stands with a cast on, pissed off and cursed, to watch my team play while I just wallowed in self pity. I had to watch my teammates run out of the famous tunnel and celebrate each other's achievements on the big "UO" on the 50-yard line. That 1991 team helped change the landscape of Sheldon football and propelled them into the powerhouse they have since become, and I wasn't a part of it.

My four-year high school career was cut down to just two. I felt robbed. I was bitter and remained that way for years to come. I was completely unfulfilled.

I was in it deep at this point. I was a crazed animal. Nothing could stop me. One month down, one to go, and I was progressing nicely.

It was not easy. After working 10-hour days in that Florida sun, I used to dread coming home to just sweat more and train. Now I fucking loved it! I couldn't wait to get off work, no matter how physically demanding it was. I demanded more from myself. My head had never been so focused.

In just a few weeks my jogging had picked up from a mile per day to almost six. My poor boxer, Drool, went from loving those little jogs and pulling me by his leash with excitement to being virtually dragged down the homestretch. I had never been so in shape in my life, and neither had my dog.

My weight-lifting sessions that used to be around an hour were now doubling in length. My body was getting tight in places I didn't know it could be. My love handles were more like love knobs now with not much left to grab.

Dieting was easier now too, and I wasn't craving sugar as much because I knew it would just detour everything I was working so hard for. This is coming from a sugar-addicted chocoholic, mind you.

I was now sprinting up the bleacher stairs at Cypress Lake High School instead of laboring up them. I would do a mile warm-up on the track, which used to be my entire cardio workout. My sprints went from a couple 40-yard dashes to 100-yard dashes and suicides on the lines.

For those who don't know what suicides are, they're called ladders now because I guess it's a more PC name. But if you really want to understand why they are and always should be called suicides, then try them for yourself. You begin at the goal line and sprint to the five-yard line, touch the line without stopping, then sprint back. Without stopping you do the same to the 10-yard line and back and then to the 15, 20, 25, 30, 35, and so on, until you get to the 50 and back. When you return back to the goal line, if you return, you want to kill yourself, hence the name suicides. It's the only name that does justice to the drill so it will forever remain in my vocabulary as such.

I went from running dozens of pass routes to hundreds of routes. I progressed from training for an hour to training until dark.

I was biking across town to get dinner rather than driving. I quit watching most TV and studied old football films, magazines, videos, and even football cards.

Training consumed my life and became who I was. I was not going to go through all this just to do it half-ass. I was going to make this team if it practically killed me, and I woke up most mornings feeling like it was.

I was a machine. I was unstoppable. I was determined.

Men live with secrets. Some are of the immoral variety and some pertain to the bottle. My secret was neither; nothing so threatening nor hurtful. My secret would have seemed stupid to anyone else who had real first-world problems, so I never shared it. Nonetheless, it tortured me frequently.

It had been well over a decade since I'd played any kind of football. I hadn't strapped on a helmet, or broken a thumb attempting to, in a dozen years.

I returned to Florida after a year of college in Oregon. I was lost but I was searching. I wasn't looking for anything particular, just a change of life, a change of pace, and hopefully, a little self-discovery.

Other than being a die-hard football fan, collector, and student of the game, I hadn't ever considered trying to play the game in an organized way again. I didn't even think it was a possibility anymore and didn't know any semi-pro leagues really existed. It was the 1990s and the Internet wasn't readily available yet to inform me of the football opportunities the world had to offer, if there even were any at that time.

I bounced around from pizza delivery boy to beach boy then back to plumber. I hated plumbing because it was all I ever did, so I often tried new things, but the money was shitty or the bosses were assholes so I always found my way back to plumbing. I played bass in a couple bands and quickly realized that I had a life full of the same old wash, rinse, and repeat. I needed more.

I found the one of many girls I slept with who wasn't a mix of psycho and slutty and could take home to meet Mom, and I proposed to her.

I think I liked the idea of settling down, getting married, and starting a grown-up life more than I wanted to get married in itself.

Jennifer was a sweet and innocent girl, but I know now that I was never head-over-heels in love with her, and after a short period I was just going through the motions of normalcy. I was just married to a good friend whom I trusted. A roommate with occasional (very occasional) benefits.

My first love was always football. No matter what I was doing, where I was living or working, or who I was with, I always found time to go to NFL games. I watched football all day on Sundays, no matter which teams were on, and I daydreamed of playing pro football.

I always reminisced about my last game of my junior year. That was all that I had. I was always bitter and sad about my lost senior season. I often wondered what could have been, although deep down I knew that nothing significant would have happened anyway. I was still too small and too slow at that point in my life. I was a late bloomer and didn't pack on bulk and body mass until the year after high school, and even though I was bigger, I still didn't have the hunger to do what it took to excel at the time.

I was in my prime, my mid-twenties, yet I still was unaware of who I really was. I knew that I wasn't where or what I wanted to be, but I didn't know how to get there or what that even was. I was still lost.

The years quickly faded by, but the feeling of my unfulfilled football career remained crystal clear. It was always there, always harassing me. It was a demon I carried with me that I just couldn't shake. Was it ridiculous, and did I have more important things to worry about? Absolutely. But that doesn't change the fact that it was something I felt passionately about, and I could not help that or fix it. I was a prisoner to my own ridiculousness.

I never told anybody this feeling; not my best friends, not even my mom whom I would tell everything to. Nobody knew about my nagging mental football madness or lack thereof. I lived with this secret my whole life. Maybe I was too embarrassed to share it with anyone.

Maybe it was because it was the only thing in my life thus far that I didn't have control over or a say about. I was an alpha male, and I didn't like to lose or lose out on anything. Football was the one thing that beat me and got the best of me and I hated that.

I often buried it in my mind and would go on with my life forgetting about it until the pre-season started back up. Then the memories would fire up again.

I was nearing 30 years old and working for my dad once again. My family had moved back to Florida in 1995 after my little brother graduated, as they'd planned. I worked for my dad in stretches until we got into an argument and I'd quit, or he fired me. It was a routine wheel we often spun, but I always ended up circling back to him. I'm not sure if it was for love or money or a little bit of both.

I was running giant crews of 20-30 guys for big contract jobs for my dad's company.

On those hot days there was nothing I looked forward to more than my lunch break. And for lunch, there was nothing I loved more than hot buffalo wings.

On one particular day that was hotter than normal, I decided to go to lunch early. I had drank a ton of water that day to survive the heat, so instead of going a few extra miles to Hooters, I pulled into Stevie Tomatoes Sports Bar because I had to piss so badly. Little did I know that that decision and that pee would change my life that day.

FROM HYENA TO HERNIA

Tryouts were only two weeks away and I was already set, both physically and mentally. It was Sunday night, and I was in the middle of a huge field workout. I felt something weird in my crotch, so I stopped my workout a little early. I wasn't horny, I didn't need to piss, so what was this? I shrugged it off and went home to take a cold shower, thinking that would help.

I had been training my ass off for nearly two months. The progress I was making was incredible. I'd completely transformed my body, which was pretty muscular from a decade of weight lifting but was, until recently, hidden behind several fluffy layers of sugary indiscretions and regular hunting for the mighty buffalo wing.

I had muscle tone that I didn't think was possible on my physique. I was cursed with the metabolism speed of a three-legged hippo, but I was fighting that beastly battle, and winning.

I was easlily jogging six miles now, four times per week, running for almost an hour straight, then coming home to lift weights. I was sprinting up bleachers in the worst heat-indexed portion of the summer days and rounding that out with 100-yard sprints, 40-yard sprints, and 100-yard suicides. I was running 50-100 pass routes and catching 90 percent of them. I was more than a machine; I was the most in-shape person I knew and more than I had ever been in my entire life, way more. I was obsessed.

My dad's company got a new job contract putting in an entirely new sewer system at a trailer park, including a water drainage system. My 10-hour days of digging ditches in the 100+ degree heat now included welding tops of steel lift station covers that weighed a ton. I was crawling under nasty, rodent-infested trailers to connect sewage pipes and tearing up asphalt drives in between them to lay culverts and storm drains.

The day was fresh. I hadn't exerted myself yet or even finished my coffee when it happened. I was walking down the drive between two rows of trailers pointing out things to my foreman that I wanted him to do that day. Suddenly I felt the sharpest pain right above my junk. I had never experienced anything like it before. It instantly stopped me in my tracks, and I dropped to my knees in agony. I crumpled to the ground, landing in an infant position with my arms between my legs clutching my groin.

My foreman freaked out and was asking what the hell was wrong and if he should call an ambulance. Of course, I was way too macho for that, but I did accept his help getting up and walking me to the car arm in arm like a wounded soldier. I managed to crawl into the car, keeping my legs as close together as possible and trying not to move my torso. I drove myself to the ER not having any damn clue what was going on with me.

"Pull down your pants," the doctor demanded. "And your underwear, son." My cock was about the size of a shiitake mushroom at this point, which normally concerns a man, and you'd pull it back out to normal size like a cow's utter. However, I didn't give two shits because I was in too much pain. The doctor immediately pointed out a giant lump in the top of my ball bag.

"See that mass?" he said. "That is a hernia." Then he examined the other side of the shaft. "See that one too? That's a double hernia." He grimaced, "You must be in a lot of pain." No shit, doc, you think. He referred me to a specialist, and it was bad enough to get me in within a couple days. I remember him saying something like, "Don't lift anything or do anything physical until your appointment." I chuckled under my breath thinking that I was having enough trouble just walking out the door and how could I do those even if I wanted to.

After surviving two of the most painful days of my life, not being able to work or workout, I saw the specialist. He showed me the X-rays and said that basically my guts had torn through the layer that holds them in place and they'd fallen into my ball bag, hitting all the tender nerves along the way. "It's probably some of the most pain a man could feel. I relate it to childbirth pain for a woman."

I asked him how this could have happened. I thought hernias were caused by lifting heavy things improperly. The doctor asked if I had been doing anything out of the ordinary lately or overdoing things.

"HAHAHA," I laughed. "You mean other than running 6 miles per day, lifting mass amounts of weights, running sprints and bleachers for hours on end for seven days a week over the last two months? Like that kind of exertion?"

"Do you wear a jockstrap or any kind of support down there during all this?" he replied. In a moment of absolute duhhhh-ness I answered no, with my head shrunk between my shoulders. I already knew what he was going to say, and a massive light bulb of clarity and stupidity instantly flicked on in my head.

"Well, that will do it," said the doc. "All that bouncing and moving made your insides bounce right through their holder and into some other parts of your insides," he explained, in much less layman terms.

What do you think my first thought and first words out of my mouth were to the doctor? If you guessed, "Will I still be able to try out for the football team in two weeks," then you guessed absolutely correct. The doctor then actually laughed out loud at me.

"Son," he said, "you need to go into surgery right away just so you can walk without pain. We have to pull your guts out of your balls and put wire mesh under them to hold them in place, so it doesn't happen again. You will barely be able to move for a week, let alone do anything physical. You will then have stitches in for two weeks and need to take it easy long after that to prevent re-injury."

"Okay," I replied. "BUT could I still try if I was willing to risk all that? Would I physically be able to?"

He said, "Technically you could, but it would be really stupid, and REALLY painful. And you'd probably end up back in my office right afterward."

Just my fucking luck. I'd trained so hard that I trained myself right into a double hernia. I had never worn a jockstrap my whole life; I was never really educated on what it was for. I'd just figured it was an extra layer of protection for when you got hit in the nuts. I didn't have any friends who wore them as kids, and it was never really discussed. Advice for youth or your kids: wear a jockstrap when training, and protect those jewels!

I was devastated. I almost got depressed, but then the sheer will power and focus that I had acquired over the last couple months, that had become a part of my nature, soon took over. I'd be damned if all that hard work I did was in vain. I wasn't going to let this injury stop me.

I got the surgery days later. When I awoke in the hospital bed, the first thing I thought of was how soon I could get back out on that field and train. I had already lost a few valuable days and my body and mind were both antsy.

I lost a couple more days before I could even walk normal. I had to walk softly, like on eggshells, just to avoid pain. It sucked! I couldn't do anything. I couldn't even lift a can of soup, let alone any weights. Tryouts were less than a week away.

Days later, I was finally walking and able to bend over enough to squat down and take a dump. I wasn't sure if taking a pain-free shit felt more like victory or adding insult to injury.

I finally went back to work, although I had to limit myself to very light duty, much to the chagrin of my dad. At least I was moving around a bit. I felt like everything I'd worked so hard for was quickly slipping away. How long does "being in shape" last without support?

I was back to work for only a few days when the day arrived. The day I'd trained so hard for, for so long. The day that had made me transform my entire body and life. Tryout day!

I was nowhere close to being ready. I was only two weeks removed from surgery and hadn't done a thing physically since then because I physically couldn't. I don't even think I had stretched my torso back to normal since my surgery. I was afraid to. I'd come so far and felt like I'd lost everything. How could I have had such bad luck when I was so dedicated to something so good?

I watched the hours come and go throughout the day as they ticked down to the start of tryouts--where I wouldn't be, where I couldn't be. Five o'clock came and I was still working in that fucking trailer park instead of working out on the practice field in front of coaches.

I was full of emotions, but unlike myself and my typical positive outlook on life, I was filled with negativity. I was pissed off, both at myself and whatever high power had allowed this to happen. I was feeling sorry for myself in a huge way—even more so than the pity I felt after my senior year injury. This was a newly discovered emotion and I hated it. I was officially depressed.

I was getting a call from a number I didn't know, so I didn't bother answering. I went back to spray-painting lines across the trailer park asphalt where my crew needed to cut up the road to lay drainage pipe.

Lunch came early that day, and I was too disenchanted in my situation to even enjoy buffalo wings. I settled for Arby's because at that point, what was the point of eating healthy?

The remainder of the day was dragging on. It was hot and I was already anxious to get home to attempt to lift weights for the first time since surgery, just to feel something productive. I'd been wondering how much strength I had lost in those two weeks down. But it was only 1:30 and I still had a long day ahead of me in the damn heat.

Buzz. There it was again, the same phone number that rang me before lunch. I decided to answer it just so I was not annoyed even more if they call again.

"Is this Chris Rohaley?"

Of course. A sales call. "Who's asking?" I said.

"This is John Torregrossa, Head Coach of the Florida Stingrays." I stopped in my tracks and picked my jaw up off the ground to find a shady spot close by.

"So, I see that you signed up for tryouts a couple months ago, but I'm not sure if you knew that we had our first tryout last night. I was wondering if you forgot or just weren't interested anymore? I am calling the few guys that didn't show up, so I know who to check off my list."

I was shocked he even knew who I was, and I thought it was very cool and professional that he was even reaching out. What I was about to tell him was one of the hardest things that I'd ever had to say.

"I can't."

"May I ask why," he said. "Is it something that I can help with?"

"I wish it was, and I wish I could tryout more than anything, trust me."

I proceeded to tell him the entire story of how much and how hard I'd trained for the opportunity and that two weeks ago I was in the best shape of my life, even at 30 years old. I then went on to tell him that it had caused a double hernia and I'd just had surgery two weeks ago, and still had my stitches in my abdomen. I had been sidelined for two weeks and probably lost all the cardio and strengthening momentum I'd been making. I told him that I had never felt depression in my life up until that point. I'm not sure why I confided in him; he just seemed like the type of guy who cared, and he really listened with a sympathetic ear.

"Well, that is so unfortunate, I am so sorry. It sounds like you were meant to play for me, I love that kind of passion," he replied.

"Passion is the one thing I never lack!"

"Well, let me ask you this, Chris, can you run right now?"

"Actually, I'm not sure. I have been too afraid to try, to be honest with you. I had never felt physical pain like I did before that surgery, so I guess it has me a little timid right now."

"I only ask because you worked so hard. I would hate to see you miss out on your dream. We won't be tackling or in pads for at least a week, so if you think you could come run drills and see how you feel, I would love to have you try."

A dramatic pause filled the phone waves. I had about three seconds to contemplate the most serious decision I'd ever had to make since putting a ring on my finger.

That decision took an entire two seconds to make.

"I'll be there tonight!" The answer just flowed out of me, like my soul wouldn't even let my brain contemplate an alternative.

There was no way after coming that far that I wasn't going to try after that coach opened my eyes. I would regret it the rest of my life, and I refuse to ever live with regret. It's just how I operate, without choice in the matter.

Torregrossa was right. As a head coach, he was already a great motivator.

I needed to get off my ass and at least try. If I tried and failed, I could accept that at this point. But if I just used my injury as an excuse, I would never forgive myself.

What was the worst that could happen? Well, actually a lot. I could re-aggravate my injury that was nowhere near fully healed yet. I could relive the excruciating pain that took me to my knees several times. I could fuck up my body, and psyche, for a long time to come and maybe never have the will to get back up. So basically, the whole thing could cause irreparable damage physically, mentally, and spiritually.

Luckily for me, I didn't think of any of those things. Self-doubt isn't a word in the Chris Rohaley dictionary. I lived my life by taking small risks and I was ready to take a big one. I wasn't going to let worry, excuses, or even logic deflate my dream.

It was about 2:00 then. That gave me three-and-a-half hours to get ready. I had to finish work, race home to get my cleats and some water, and get to the practice field across town. Coincidentally it was my home field that I had been training at for the last two months, so that was already in my favor. I felt comfortable there.

I had to crush this tryout. I already didn't want to let the coach down. I was a day behind the rest of the guys, so I had some catching up to do, but I wasn't about to let that dampen my spirits.

DAY 1

Nothing like running a jack hammer, welding torch, and plate compactor all day, then dashing off to get to your first semi-professional tryout in time without a spare minute to eat, shit, or shower in between.

I had to change into my gym shorts in the car at a stoplight and replace my dirty work boots for dirty cleats when I got to the parking lot of the practice field. I didn't have time for the anxiety to catch up with me nor the room in my brain for it to even exist--I was too focused. I just hoped that I would do well enough during the next week that this rushing and changing in the car would be a constant issue. It would be an inconvenience I actually hoped to have.

I pulled into my normal stomping grounds, the field where I had been leaving my heart and sweat for the last two months before my surgery. It was quite different this time because I could barely find a parking space.

I was completely nervous, but not really about competing. It was more about if my guts were going to fall into my ball bag again or if I was going to dislodge some wire mesh to float around in places it shouldn't be floating around, toxifying my body.

When I got to the field I was in shock. There were over 90 players there. Holy shit! I guess a lot of young guys had a similar dream as I did or at least were trying to advance their current football situations. When I say young, I emphasize young! I felt like the old grandpa of the group among all those baby-faced ballers.

"Hi Mr. Torregrossa, I'm Chris Rohaley."
"Coach will do fine. Thanks for coming out to try. I'm glad you're here, but please be careful Chris."

We both knew that I couldn't do that if I was to make this team. It was quite the opposite. I had to take every risk possible and push myself to the edge of emotional distress, the brink of exhaustion, and the threshold of pain tolerance, combined with a little praying and a lot of luck. The whistle blew and we got the order to do a couple laps and fall in for stretching. It was 101 degrees outside at the heat climax of the day, with zero breeze for relief.

Here we go. I had done little more than take a shit for exercise in the last couple weeks and now I was going to run alongside 90 guys in top shape and try to keep up. Trial by fire--and when I say fire, I mean that my guts and nuts were actually on fire, burning with pain already.

I finished the warm-up jog and fell in formation to stretch. Bending over to touch my toes killed. Stretching my elbow above my head killed. Everything hurt! I noticed a dark spot out of the bottom of my eye. I looked down to find that my stitches had already opened. I was bleeding through my shorts. We weren't even five minutes deep into practice, and I was already questioning my resolve.

I was out of breath too. I felt like the two weeks of down time after surgery had also killed my cardiovascular reserves. My tank was empty. How could I have lost so much so quickly? I felt completely out of shape and out of sorts. My mind was starting to defeat my spirit. I had to stop it, and now!

Chris, quit being a god-damn pussy, I told myself. You trained too hard and long for this. I had to Yoda myself up. Just remember your training. You got this, you got this! I forced my thoughts onto a different path. Show all these kids why they need to respect you. More importantly, prove to yourself that you can do this. Don't let yourself down no matter how much it hurts. You only get this one chance; make the most of it. The pain will heal but the success or failure will last forever--your choice which one it will be.

I gave myself the pep talk I needed, and it worked. I was ready. I was ready. I told myself to find a place in my mind where I could ignore the pain and the blood.

We ran some basic cone drills that I had been running since the fourth grade. I'd spent my whole life hating those damn cone drills, even dreading them during warm-ups. Now I loved every second of them. I was grateful to be on the same patch of grass as these cones. There was no place else on earth I would've rather been than right there, right then. I made those pointy, orange rubber things my bitch. I was hurting but the pain was dull in comparison to my spirit. I got my balls back, and they felt bigger than they had ever been.

After cone and agility drills, the coaches broke us off into position drills.

"Receivers, come with me," the slender coach said from across the field. I ran to join the group.

"Hey, man, you're bleeding," the coach said to me when I got closer.

"I'm all good, no worries." I shrugged it off in a moment of super-toughness and bad-assery.

Why I still had being a receiver stuck in my head I had no idea, especially since I had so much success at linebacker, albeit very briefly, the last time I actually played organized ball in high school. Maybe it was because that is what I was trying out for my senior year before I lost the opportunity to injury. Or maybe it was because my entire football philosophy and motivation was molded after my idol, Steve Largent, and somehow, I felt I owed it to his inspiration to at least try and be a receiver. Whatever it was, I was in over my head.

My routes were spot-on, and my hands were the best of the whole lot, but my speed was, well, nonexistent. I was slow taking off and slower once I got going. I was like a crippled Wile E. trying to keep up with a bunch of roadrunners. I did as best as I could, even making some spectacular diving catches. However, if I'd had the speed to catch up to those balls, I wouldn't have needed to dive for them in the first place. With every dive I wondered if I would get up in more pain or even get up at all.

Practice came to conclusion, and we all started walking toward our cars. I felt like I'd done good, but was it good enough to get noticed? I hung in there and didn't let my injury slow me down, and I was proud of that. I told the coach thanks for talking me into coming and that I would see him tomorrow.

I got to my car and melted into the seat. That's when the adrenaline began to fade away and the reality of my surgery started resurfacing with a vengeance. I looked down and had two perfect bloodstains on my shirt and shorts. The blood had soaked through both layers. I dreaded pulling everything up to see what kind of mess I'd caused. I was petrified. I decided to drive home and deal with it then in the shower. What I needed most then was a gallon of water and a pile of buffalo wings. I felt like I'd definitely earned them, and I hadn't had any in months.

DAY 2

What I feared would happen absolutely did. My skin had torn through my stitches from practice and my surgery cuts were opened. I told myself to be a man and deal with it. Each are only a couple inches big, quit being a baby.

My dad could be a real hard ass, and he wouldn't let me go to the doctor to get my wounds sewn back up AND take off early for practice. So, I chose to skip the first and do the latter. I'd have time to go home and get cleaned up and a second to take a breath before tryouts resumed. I'd need a little downtime to cool off and take a cold shower. I had it all planned out.

Work decided not to agree with my perfect plan. When you oversee an entire crew, awaiting inspectors and deliveries, and have deadlines, you can't just end work when it's convenient for you. I cared about my job. I mean, it did have my family name attached to it, so I took pride in the work being well done. Everyone was running late all day and it caught up with me. It looked like I would be changing in the car again on the way to the field.

Since I couldn't go home to take care of my injury, I had to do it on the fly with the tools I had at hand on a work truck. What's the best replacement for stitches? I could only think of one thing. It's one of mankind's greatest inventions ever, and every man should have it readily available at all times: duct tape!

I ripped off two four-inch pieces and placed them right on my skin over my wounds. Perfect! That would hold. Wait, I'd better put a longer piece over top both, so the sweat doesn't loosen them. There, that's better. All set to go get tackled by grown men.

My second day at camp felt a little better. I went into it mentally prepared, giving my mind little chance to fuck with my heart. The duct tape kept the bleeding at bay, and although I still had a muscle-soreness hangover from day #1, I was loosening up quickly. Hard to believe I wasn't even two weeks removed from the operating table, and I was actually doing it. I knew that I wasn't anywhere near my 100 percent, but I could operate at 70 percent and make up the other 30 percent in heart and hustle.

We broke into our position groups even quicker than the day before. I think the coaching staff was eager to make final assessments since they only had a week before they had to make cuts.

Head Coach Torregrossa called a couple guys over who were obviously out of shape and out of their league while the rest of us started our routes. I couldn't help but notice instant downtrodden expressions of defeat and failure on their faces as they hung their heads low and made the long, lonely journey back to their cars for the last time. We all knew what that was. They were cut. After three days, the staff already knew they weren't cut out to be professional football players. We all knew it already too, but nobody wants to talk about it during camp, cause you could be next.

I was just glad it wasn't me . . . until it was me! When Coach Torregrossa called me over next, my heart just dropped. Already? Holy shit this isn't fair. I didn't even get to prove my worth in pads yet. I was sick to my stomach before even taking the first step toward him. It was the longest 15 yards that I'd ever ran on a football field.

"Chris, I'm so glad you tried out," Coach said, starting the worst conversation I could ever imagine. "I talked to Coach Fain, the receivers coach, and he said that he wished everyone had your route running and hands, but you are simply too slow to compete at that position."

"I understand," I replied sheepishly, already mentally preparing myself for the inevitable.

"However," Torregrossa continued, "Fain said you have the most heart and best hustle on the team. He said that you were unbreakable, and I tend to agree after knowing about what you are out here doing, right after your surgery with stitches still in and all. That takes courage and demands respect. We all feel that way."

"Well, thanks, it hasn't been easy, but then again, it's football, and if it was easy, it wouldn't be such a great game, right?"

"Absolutely right. And that's why . . ."

There it was, the moment I was dreading. Well, at least they know

I gave it my all, and I know it. Nobody could ever take that away from me.

"We decided you would be much better suited to try out with the linebackers because of your hands and size."

Wait, what?! Did he just say I wasn't cut yet? Not only was I not cut, but he was giving me a second chance at the position I was meant to play anyway. I was ecstatic. Some guys might have been offended or let their egos puff up and inflate this scenario. Not me! I was relieved and felt blessed. The fact alone that the coaches noticed me after a lifetime of playing a sport where I wasn't sure if half my coaches even knew my name or position, felt phenomenal. The coaches respected me and saw my heart. That's all I needed. That was my foot in the door. Now it was time to slam that fucker open.

"I would love to do that, Coach. That's actually my natural position from high school." A bit of a stretch, but hey, I was pulling out all and any cards by that point.

"Sounds great, I'm excited to see what you can do on defense," said the coach. "You're a few days behind now so you'll have some catching up to do."

"I'm not worried about that," I said confidently. "I know that position like none other." Another stretch, but I did have great football instincts, and I was confident those would replace any lack of experience or shortcomings that I had at the position.

I got involved in the last few drills with the linebacker core that was about 10 guys deep at that point. I definitely had a lot to prove and a lot of guys to beat out. I was once again the underdog and had to prove my heart, will, and bark all over again to a new set of coaches who knew nothing about me. This wasn't going to be easy. But by that point I was so used to "not easy" it didn't faze me. Adversity was my middle name.

DAY 3

Day three for me was actually the fourth day of tryouts since I'd missed the first day. I had today and one more day to prove myself and make the team.

I was two days behind as far as the linebacker core was concerned and had a tall mountain of competition to climb. I had to get noticed somehow. The coaches needed to know what I was going through--and what I went through--to get there.

There were fewer faces on the field that day. Maybe 75-80 guys instead of 90. Coaches must have called some guys to tell them not to bother to return. It was definitely a noticeable change. Time for the cream to rise to the top, and I was still curdling way down at the bottom of the bowl.

We still weren't in pads. I'm sure they were saving those for once the team was set. There's no way they'd had the budget for 90 sets of pads anyway. I would have to prove myself without showing how I could hit. Which was fine because I hadn't had full contact with another player in over a decade and wasn't sure how I was going to fare at it, surgery or not. Oddly enough, I wasn't too worried about it at that point, though. One thing at a time. I had to make this team first.

Positions were starting to get decided and coaches already had their favorites. The coaches ran me hard over and over. I think they were testing my will. My fortitude was strong; they wouldn't be able to break me.

I got in at regular rotations at outside linebacker because the middle linebacker was definitely set with Seth at the helm. Seth was a horse, a Clydesdale of a man. How this dude wasn't starring in college was beyond me. I'd hate to go against him if I were a running back. It made me wonder just how phenomenal the athletes actually were in the NFL if this guy couldn't make the cut.

Before I knew it, I was making quicker breaks on the ball and getting to the coach faster on blitzes. What really stood out were my hands in drills. I was catching everything low and high, balls that other guys were either dropping or not getting to. All that practice at receiver the last couple of months was paying off.

By the end of practice, my playing rotations in drills shifted to middle linebacker behind Seth, The Horse. I was making an impression quickly. I ran when other guys walked to the huddle. I bounced up after I fell, when other guys were slow to rise. I clinched my guts in pain in between plays and drills but set that shit aside when the whistle blew.

When The Horse started talking to me and giving me small compliments, that's when I knew I was doing something right. You need to earn respect on the field, no matter who you are or where you come from. The football field is the one place where all gladiators are equal at the start of practice. Race, color, nationality, background, money--none of that crap matters in competition to make a team. It's all about skill, heart, and work ethics. I definitely had the last two in spades, and The Horse saw that, and he respected that.

Others must have started noticing too.

DAY 4 - Last Day of Tryouts

When I stepped on the field it was a little thinner. The crowd of 75-80 was maybe down to 60 souls now. My linebacker coach came directly over to me with another coach whom I hadn't yet met. He introduced me to his peer.

"Chris, this is John, the tight end coach. John, this is the guy I was telling you about who started as a receiver and moved over to linebacker. The guy with the bleeding stitches who just had surgery."

Apparently, the word had spread and the whole coaching staff now knew of my predicament. What I thought was an ailment holding me back was becoming a blessing in disguise. As long as I could hold the pain at bay, not run out of duct tape, and stay healthy, I might actually have a run at this.

"Nice to meet you, Chris," John said. "Craig, the linebacker coach, told me about your hands and your hustle and thought you might be useful as a tight end substitute as well. I already have my starter, Morgan, but I need a reliable backup. Would you want to try and play both ways a little?"

Apparently, my hustle and hands were also making a good impression among the coaching staff. Funny how heart and hustle can get you noticed as easily as actual talent and speed.

"I would love too!"

"Okay, great. Well, we will split up your time between the two. Why don't you come over with me for now and let's see what you got."

I lined up with just a few other guys. The biggest of the bunch was named Morgan Halle. The other couple guys looked like they'd just left the bar or the couch and were panting like dogs. I could see why Morgan needed a reliable backup. I was happy to show them up in mere seconds.

Morgan Halle should have been a pro. He looked like one and played like one. He carried himself like a pro and was a born leader. Halle was 6'4" and 250 lb., just a beast. In 1989 he was 1st Team All-State as a tight end at Candor High in NY. After a couple years at community college, he'd gotten a scholarship to Clemson University but sadly missed his window of opportunity with a bad shoulder injury. Now, the 28-year-old landscaper production manager was trying to mount a comeback for a second shot at glory, kind of like yours truly. Although, his chances were way better than mine. I just wanted to make the team.

Block the bag and peel out for a 5-and-out route. Cake. I hit the bag hard and turned my head immediately to find the coach trying to surprise me, even test me, with a quick throw. It didn't faze me. I caught it, and every single one after it, thanks to a lifetime of Steve Largent inspiration and emulation.

"Nice grab," said Morgan The Clemson Tiger. He immediately talked to me. You know what that meant: respect. I think he knew that I was going to be his understudy. He had zero reason to worry about me taking his job away AND he knew that I would be better for the team than those other scrubs in line behind us.

"Thanks, dude," was my signature response. I called everybody "dude," but the inflection in my voice determined if he was really THE dude or just a dude. Morgan knew which one he was.

Well, that practice was sure a step in the right direction. But was it enough? I made some good impressions with coaches and a couple new friends in The Horse and The Tiger. I was feeling pretty good, at least mentally.

My body on the other hand wasn't handling things as well. I was hanging on by a thread physically. My abdomen killed me to even breath heavy and was just getting worse. I was afraid to even think about what kind of new damage I'd caused. My muscles were so sore I could barely move them at nights, and my job with my dictator boss didn't allow for any time to get massages or any rest. My shins had started hurting from all the hard running. I think it was the onset of shin splints. Remember, I was probably 8-10 years older than most of those guys and my body didn't bounce back like those younger bucks'. I was a wreck.

But none of that mattered now because I'd made it through. I'd had four days of absolute torture. Four days to prove myself among 90 other guys trying to do the same thing, yet I was older than most all of them. I went through every emotion possible, even discovering some new ones along the way. I felt pain that I'd never felt in my life and endured more than I'd ever thought possible.

Now I had the weekend to rest my body, but there would be no relaxing my mind. I would be anxiously waiting for my phone to ring to see if I'd done enough to make my dream come true or if I just didn't have what it took. I was ready to accept my fate and proud in the fact that I'd finally had my opportunity to leave it all on the field. I'd given it my all and left blood, sweat, and tear-stained grass out there between the uprights.

COACHES CALL II

The phone rang. My heart pounded through my chest. To say that this call didn't mean everything to me would be a total lie. This one call was a culmination of two months of pain and perseverance. This call would define me and what I was capable of.

I could barely muster a squeaky hello.

"Chris?"

It was Coach Torregrossa. His voice would be forever implanted in my brain now regardless of the outcome of this conversation.

"Yes, Coach."

"How you feeling tonight?"

"I'm great, Coach. A little sore, but otherwise good." That was a total lie.

"I was just calling my players to tell them the practice schedule for next week and when equipment checkouts are."

"Wait, does that mean I'm one of your players?" I was in shock. Did I hear that right? Was that his way of saying I made the team?

"Yes, it does, Chris. Welcome to the Florida Stingrays, we are glad to have you."

If one can simultaneously shit his pants, jump for joy, scream at the top of his lungs inside without making a sound, and have his mind blown, then I just did all that. And more.

"Oh man, thank you so much, Coach. I won't let you down I promise." It took every constraint I had to reply like a man and not a giddy little girl. I had to get off this phone before I exploded.

"I know you won't let us down. You made this team because nobody showed the heart and both mental and physical toughness that you did. You are an inspiration to others and an example of how we want our players to be. A true leader."

"Thanks so much, Coach. You have no idea what that means to me to hear. I wanted this more than anything."

"I could tell," Coach replied. "See you on Monday."

I dropped the phone and ran circles around the house like I was three years old again. I was so happy I cried. I actually wept like a baby.

I did it. I really did it.

The day had finally arrived. After a weekend of rest and recovery, my body was ready to get abused once again, but this time it was for real. Not only was I really a part of the Florida Stingrays semi-professional football team, but we were about to really hit each other in pads at full speed. This is where the boys got separated from the men, the big dicks from the little pussies.

We met at the school, and Coach Torregrossa opened his van to reveal piles of old pads from every year, make, and model you could imagine. It was more of a hodge podge of foam and plastic, but it would do, and nobody who just made this team was complaining.

I was nearly last in line since I'd had to bolt over straight from work, so I was left with what I could barely refer to as leftovers. My shoulder pads were about two sizes too big and my practice pants about one size too small. Luckily my helmet fit great, but there was no way this thing could've been approved for full contact anymore. The interior pads were old and just foam. No air, no suspension; this was old-school hard knocks football. Back then, there was no governing body to check helmet integrity, and nobody yet knew much about concussions and chronic traumatic encephalopathy, or CTE, which wasn't yet a thing.

No matter. I didn't think twice about it. This was what I wanted more than anything, and I was grateful to wear that old clunker on my old dome.

What I cared most about was getting the correct number on my jersey. There was only one number that would work for me. Only one number punctuated the whole reason why I was even standing there. I yelled it out and the coach threw me a jersey. Was it that easy? Did the football gods shine on me yet again? As I untangled the white, silver and black silky-smooth uniform I saw it; first an eight, then a zero. After all that I had been through to get to this point it was only right that I slipped that number over my chest. Now it was official.

Coach Torregrossa gave us a speech filled with grandeur and lofty promises. We were going to get paychecks after every game.

"This is pro ball, boys. You get paid to play pro ball," Coach answered a pondering from the crowd. "We have a game in the Bahamas too," Coach continued. "You will each get game tickets to sell to help our cause and fill the stands, which by the way will be full of pro scouts." Gasps were heard from the group. "That's right. This isn't some lame 9 vs. 9 league full of high schoolers who couldn't make a junior college team. We have former college starters on our team. We will be playing teams with former NFL flunkies and filled with guys who got cut in the final days of training camps looking to prove they belong at the top, at any cost. This is no joke. Welcome to the big time that may get you to the biggest time."

Then we all broke for the first full-contact practice with dreams of glory and the coach's slick words pumping through our veins like a shot of adrenaline.

BAM! My first hit was felt out on Cypress Lake Blvd. And I was the tackler! Hitting Morgan was like hitting a brick wall. I got him down on the ground, but boy did I feel it, and I would continue to later that night.

Hitting at this level was a lot different than in high school, which had been the last time I'd hit or gotten hit by anybody. We were children then. Now we were grown, mature men hitting each other with zero regard for personal safety, full of focused ambition for football glory that drove our power through every tackle. In high school, we hit because we had to and the coach told us to. Now we hit because we'd dreamed of it and the bigger things that could come from it the harder we did it.

I was far better at this than I ever was before. I was a different man now than I was way back then. I was actually a man, not a scared, timid boy. I used to pull back just a little with every tackle. I was the receiver of the collision; now I was the initiator. I gave every tackle 110 percent and was so much better for it. Letting go of fear is an exhilarating feeling and opens up your entire game. It allows you to do great things. It also opens you up for more injury, but if you fear getting hurt, you are in the wrong game. Time to go play soccer.

I was part of a team again and it felt so sweet. I didn't just have new teammates--I had a band of 40 brothers. I was rapidly getting close to several of them. Every guy had a completely unique background and a story that led him to this field of battle. In fact, the tales were so interesting that I realized it was part of our image and allure. I wanted everyone to know about them. We were a band of fathers, misfits, forgotten, or overlooked. We were young and old and every shape, size, and color in between. I needed to share this with family, friends, and fans, it was too interesting not to.

I asked Coach Torregrossa if I could somehow tell the story about us publicly. I wanted fans in the stands to put a history and backstory to the names of the guys they were watching. I figured what better way than doing a newsletter or program for each game.

I called it The Stinger. I included a roster and news in each issue. There was a recap of the prior week's game and a couple different players or a coach profiled that I had gotten to know and bond with during practices.

Morgan and I were fast friends by this point, so I naturally had to tell his story in the first issue, followed by Seth Petruzelli, the hard-hitting horse of a linebacker from Cape Coral.

Seth had been a 1st Team All-State center from Mariner High School and was trying to get noticed by scouts. The 19 year old was solid muscle and built like a brick shit house. I wouldn't have wanted to be a quarterback with this guy running me down. Seth, who could bench press over 400 lb., might have looked intimidating, but you never saw him not smiling and having fun.

Then there was Billy Bryan. BB reminded me of the character Sunshine from Remember the Titans. He looked like he was fresh off the beach with his long, blond, surfer-like hair protruding from under his helmet. Billy immediately started at safety because he would just throw his whole body into tackles without fear or any regard for personal safety.

Kenny Wigfalls looked like he'd been scoring touchdowns his whole life. #3 was born to be a receiver. He was fast and shifty, and I hated trying to catch him to tackle him.

Our kicker looked more like an out-of-shape former offensive guard. Phil Setterquist was a 230-pound dude who might have been as old as me, or older. With his belly flopping out from under his jersey, he looked like he was the last person who belonged on the football field. But when he booted that ball, people soon forgot his unathletic physique and noticed his incredibly strong leg. He had a cannon for a foot. Later, Phil went on to kick for the new expansion Florida Firecats of the Arena Football League after his time as a Stingray.

At quarterback was not only our team captain, but our team owner, Lester Burnette. Burnette is another name remembered by local fans. In the 1980s, Lester beat out future NFL Hall of Famer Deion Sanders as the starting quarterback at North Ft. Myers High. Burnette had played for the Stingrays before, when they were a minor league team in the Florida Football League from 1991-93. That team got sold and moved to Venice, and its history had remained buried in an old garage until Burnette recovered and resurrected it. He bought the rights from the old owner and revamped the team's image and brand.

Richard Fain was the defensive backs coach. If that name sounds familiar in Florida, it's because many local fans remember him from starring at North Ft. Myers High, and many national fans remember him from his All-American senior year as a Florida Gator. Drafted in the 6th round by the Cincinnati Bengals, Fain played four seasons in the NFL with the Bengals, Bears, and Redskins.

It's because of Burnette's hard work and passion that I got the chance to make this dream of mine become reality. I don't know where he is today, but I want to thank him for all that he did.

The day I got my jersey and pads. Shoulder pads too big, pants too small, helmet too old < Me too happy! I ended up taking a hacksaw to the top middle bar portion in face-mask because I felt it looked too much like a lineman's face-mask.

I had never been involved in anything like this before. The team did press and promotion leading up to the season opener. We visited local businesses to push our tickets and get support. We even had an autograph signing at our huge local shoe/sports store, Just For Feet. Morgan, Seth, Lester, and a few other guys and I sat at a table in the middle of the store and signed photos for kids and encouraged them to stay in school and try hard at football so they could be sitting in our seats one day.

Did I mention that I was also the team photographer? I wrote the official team program and asked Burnette if I could also be the official photographer. I had been the Ft. Myers Miracle minor league baseball team photographer the previous season, and it was another passion of mine. I offered my services for free just to help out the team. Burnette saw my passion and portfolio and was all for it. He could tell that I was also passionate about his team, and other than maybe Morgan, who was our player representative, nobody did more to help support his dream.

We had been practicing our asses off for the last month, selling game tickets around town, and making promotional appearances. We were ready. Bring on game #1!

Game 1 vs. Texas Diablos

Our first game was at home against the Texas Diablos on August 28, 1999. It was doomed from the start. In the week leading up to the game, the rains started in Texas. Instead of letting up, they got worse and worse until the flooding began. Hurricane Brett wreaked havoc in Texas and the Corpus Christie team couldn't make the trip. The game was postponed until the end of the season.

The moment I had been waiting so long for, the moment I had dreamed of was washed away from me in an instant. I was so bummed out, and the anxiousness would have to build for yet another week. I was about to explode. I had to redirect my attention elsewhere. So, I connected with some teammates and conducted some interviews for my Stinger game program. I'd had one all set for the inaugural game, but since it got cancelled, I went back to the drawing board. I had never written anything other than a poetry book, so it was an exciting new endeavor for me. I was a 30-year-old rookie at both semi-pro football and sports writing.

On a positive note, we started off the season 1-0. Since the Diablos couldn't show, it was considered a forfeit.

The week took forever dragging along until our next game. At least I had practice to look forward to in the evenings. Still, our first game couldn't come fast enough.

Game 2 vs. Alabama Raiders

Finally, my moment had come. It was September 4, 1999, and I'd just stepped foot into the locker room way early for my first game. I thought for sure that I would be the first one there, but of course Morgan arrived before me. He must have spent the night in that musty, stank-ass room because I was three hours early and he looked like he'd been there a while.

We were playing the Alabama Raiders. I knew nothing about them. I don't think anyone did. We just knew that they'd agreed to travel to our house to play us. That's all we needed to know. We were ready. I was ready. I was also nervous as shit. In fact, I can't recall the last time I'd been this nervous. This was like wedding day what-the-fuck-am-I-about-to-do scale of nervous.

Morgan could feel it and gave me a little pep talk.

"Just do what you were meant to do, what you've been dreaming of, dude. You worked way too hard to get here through so much pain.

You got this. This is easy for you."

I looked up to Morgan and respected him. I was his backup, and a year older, but that didn't matter one bit to me. He was an amazing football player--and man. His words resonated with me and truly helped.

Our team owner and president showed up next, but today he wasn't the boss; he was just our quarterback and captain. The three of us talked while one by one the other guys filtered in. Some played hip hop in their locker, some metal, and some just sat in silent prayer or meditation while they were getting ready. It was a bruised-up bouquet of all walks of life and flavors of color, preparing for battle together.

Time was drawing closer and closer. I peeked out of the locker room field to see if the stands were filling up yet. They actually were. It was mostly family at that point. My wife and mom were already in the stands waiting in the heat.

There was just one problem. There was no sign of Alabama. Where were the Raiders? Burnette had started pacing around a little, making several calls with frustrated-looking outcomes. This wasn't looking good. Where the hell were our opponents? I saw panic in Burnette's face, and he couldn't hide it.

The crowd was getting restless outside, and the game start time had come and gone, yet nobody was on the field.

Nobody knew what was going on until Coach Torregrossa finally entered the locker room. I knew immediately that my first professional football game was not going to happen today . . . again.

"Well, guys," the coach spoke up, and the room immediately silenced. "Alabama is a no show. We have called and called everyone involved and nobody knows what happened or why they aren't answering. No signs of them anywhere. Their team bus is gone but nobody knows where." The room gasped and some f-bombs were dropped hard. "It's okay, though. Our family and fans out there came to watch football, so we are going to give them a football game. The refs are staying, and the concessions are open. We are going to play first-team offense against first-team defense. We will make the most of it and consider this a warm-up game, which we could all use."

Needless to say, we were devastated. But we were there to play football and football was what we still got to play. We were going to make the most of it and put on a good showing for the sweating fans outside braving the elements to watch us.

We all picked up our pride and our helmets and exited the locker room as a team.

The defense got black jerseys to put over our uniforms. I was one of the few players who had to take mine off and on since I was the first backup in rotation at tight end on offense and the same at linebacker on defense.

Morgan got the passing plays on offense, of course, and I was delegated to the blocking tight end plays. I didn't care though; I was playing football again. Sure, it wasn't as all-out as we were wanting to play, but we played because we loved the game regardless.

I got more playing time on defense and was seeing more time at outside linebacker than the starter. I was in on several tackles and feeling great.

Then, at the close of the first quarter, the unthinkable happened.

Our starting receiver Kenny Wigfalls got tackled on the other side of the field while making an awkward cut. His knee bent 90 degrees the wrong way and he lay in the grass in agony. He got carried off the field with a torn ACL and would be out for the season, maybe his career. That was a huge blow to the team, and a horrible loss to suffer during a practice game of all things.

I think some players questioned if it was worth it, and thought it was a waste. I disagree. We all know the risks out on that field. We play the game because it's dangerous and a rush, and not for the weak. The risk is what makes it great and exciting. Anything can happen at any moment no matter how big or badass you are. We did, in fact, need the game-situation practice; everyone can use that. I know that I needed it more than I'd thought.

I thought I was getting back in shape, but boy was I wrong. There is "being in shape" and then there is "being in football game-time shape." They are vastly different. Adrenaline only lasts so long on the field of play before you need to back it up with stamina. I could run all night long at full speed in practice and be fine, but in the game, you kick it into overdrive and find that extra gear. That extra gear wears your ass out fast! When you chase a receiver in practice you are chasing your friend. When you chase a ball carrier in a game you are chasing the enemy, so you naturally run fast and put more energy into it without even realizing it--hence, football shape.

The game wound to a close. Besides Kenny's injury, I was very happy with the outcome. I thought we performed well as a team, and I was excited to see what we could do against the enemy.

Personally, I was happy with how I did but knew that I had a ways to go to get in better football game-time shape. I was in on at least a good dozen tackles, and I saved a punt return that broke loose from scoring by running down the ball carrier at the correct angle of pursuit, which is not an easy task, especially with a fast little fucker.

Physically I was exhausted but mentally I was more ready than

Old #80 shedding blocks and eyeing his prey during Stigrays team scrimmage game 9/4/99.

STINGRAYS

ever. Bring on Atlanta!

We were 2-0 without playing a single down.

Game 3 vs. Atlanta Rage

I arrived at the stadium early again, this time even beating Morgan. I really enjoyed the quiet time alone to reflect on where I was and how far I'd come. I soaked it in.

When Morgan arrived, I immediately got nervous because I saw the intesity in his eyes. This was finally it, the real deal. Maybe it was because it had been building for several weeks now and there was extra time for the anxiety demon to surface, or maybe it was just because we'd heard that this Atlanta team was no joke. Either way, I even saw nerves on Morgan's demeanor. It was contagious.

Other players arrived and I barely noticed. Morgan and I sat by each other, trying to pump each other up and help one another out. I excused myself to go to the bathroom to shit. I always had to shit before every game even if I already had before leaving the house. The nerves magically made more shit surface. Then I puked. Not from the smell of my shit, although it was a barf-worthy dump, but I had to get my nerves out in another way. They spewed out of all ends. It actually helped.

Morgan called me over.

"Here, my man, try some of these. They will pump you up." He handed me some Yellow Jackets. If you don't remember Yellow Jackets, they were black and yellow pills packed with the stimulant ephedra. They gave you a rush like the feeling of chugging caffeine, but they lasted longer. They actually made your heart feel like it was pounding out of your chest, and I think it did in some guys, which was why they were banned by the FDA. Once reports of people dying from taking too much ephedra came out, I immediately stopped. But we didn't know the dangers then. We each took a handful and ran out onto the field like some wild fucking banshees.

Legend had quickly spread during warmups of the Rage's star running back. Rumor had it that he was cut from an NFL camp because of some serious legal issues. I don't remember his name, but I do remember that the legend of his greatness was not overexaggerated.

The beating began immediately as the Rage won the coin toss and elected to receive. Their first play was a sweep to the right and their star back took it 80 yards to the house with ease. If we didn't contain this dude, we were in for a long game.

After we'd failed to produce any points, the Rage got the ball back quickly. On their first play they handed the ball off to their superstar on a dive up the middle. Then the unthinkable happened, again. We didn't lose the play to another fast break. We lost Seth to a broken leg.

Our defensive captain and starting middle linebacker had a horrible collision and broke his femur. The femur is the longest and strongest bone in your body and breaking it can be so severe and traumatic that one can actually die from it. My friend lay in pain, and for the first time I saw no smile on his face, only fear. It seemed like eternity for the ambulance to come take him away. I wanted to go with him, but it wasn't my battle. I would be there for him whenever he needed me, but I had to be here for the rest of my team right now.

Then it happened. I was so concerned with my friend's well-being that until the coach summoned me, I didn't realize that I was next up in line. I was the backup middle linebacker.

Coach Torregrossa put his arm around me. "Chris, listen to me. You need to brush that off. I need you now, the team needs you now. You know this defense better than anyone. You need to go be our middle linebacker, our captain. You need to go lead the defense."

"Of course, Coach, I got this," and I sprinted out to the awaiting huddle. I didn't get nervous, I wasn't scared. I had a moment of total clarity. On that run from the sidelines to the huddle, my whole career passed before my eyes. Everything that I had dreamed of and strived for had led to this moment.

I had gone from a 30-year-old plumber who hadn't played ball in a dozen years and was fresh off double hernia surgery to the starting middle linebacker and captain of the defense calling plays in the huddle of a professional football team. Anyone who says that you can't manifest your own destiny has never met me! The reason that I was standing in that spot was not because of luck or circumstance. It was because I'd willed myself to be there, and I never gave up. It was unfortunate that my friend got injured and I was in the spot that he too had earned, but anybody could have taken his place. I was the next most qualified and who the coach wanted to lead the team. I alone gave the coach that confidence in me and earned his trust through my work ethic and heart. He could have called on anybody else but didn't.

I called the play, which pulled the safeties up closer to protect against the run and had the middle linebacker blitzing up the middle to stuff the hole against another dive.

Wow, my first play in professional football, and I got to blitz up the middle. Was I dreaming? I made eye contact with the QB and he looked worried. I felt like if he didn't hand off to his all-world running back, he really didn't know what to do. That running back was the identity of this Rage team, not the quarterback. That quarterback was mine. I just knew it. If he didn't hand off, he was mine.

The QB yelled out the cadence and the ball was snapped. He took a three step drop and faked the ball to his running back. I didn't fall for it. The back chose the wrong gap and went to help block on the opposite side of the center, and he didn't see me. The center shifted left to pick up one defensive tackle and the guard shifted right to pick up the other one. It left the perfect hole for me.

I had a split second to get through it before anyone noticed me. I sprinted faster than I ever had before. My shoulder pads skimmed the sides of some flailing arms but otherwise I was untouched. The quarterback was in my sights. He wasn't even looking at me, he was looking downfield to pass. They thought they could fool us with a pass because we were expecting their star back to get it again. I wasn't fooled. I was about two steps away when the QB caught a glimpse of me at the last second and shifted his feet to scramble away. He stepped up to try and slip by my bull rush, but he was too late. I hit him low, and I hit him hard. My shoulder landed right above his belt and I drove him back several feet, landing on top of him with all my force.

I got up and had to question reality for a second. It wasn't until my teammates started smacking my ass and high fiving me until I realized what I had just done. I got my sack! I just got my sack that I had dreamed of since high school, and I did it as a 30-year-old rookie in professional football. This was the greatest moment of my life. Better than marriage, better than sex--this was football glory. Those other moments come and go but this one would never fade. This moment would last forever.

My first game as a pro, on my first play, I got the sack I had longed for. It made everything I had done and been through so worth it. I would do it all again in a heartbeat, and I would not change a thing. I truly believe that the hardship and tests that I had to go through are what made it such a magical moment. No matter what else happened from this point forward, nobody could take that play away from me.

That might have been the last play we had to cheer about, though. I played every down the rest of the game and even got in on a couple tight end plays. The Rage's running back ended up rushing for over 300 yards. I had never seen anything like it. We just couldn't stop him no matter what we tried. He single-handedly kicked our ass.

We were 2-1.

Game 4 vs. Eight-Mile Crushers

With the cancellation of our first game vs. Texas and the no-show asshole Alabama Raiders, our team was severely in the hole. We relied on ticket, merch, and concession sales from every game to fund the team's overhead and get us through the season.

The players all agreed to not take a salary to help the cause. I don't think any of us were there for a paycheck. We might have lost a couple guys because of that, but we didn't want those kinds of small-visioned players on our team anyway, so fuck em!

Our sacrifice wasn't enough. The team just did not have the money to send us on the road to play. Poor Lester Burnette tried and tried, but we couldn't bring it all together in time. We had to postpone the September 18th game and try and make it up later.

We were all bummed-out about it, but we understood. We wanted revenge for the Atlanta game more than anything, and we wanted to take it out on Eight-Mile. It would have to wait.

At least we'd have two weeks to practice now and try to correct our run defense and lack of offense.

We were still 2-1.

We were being run hard. We were being taught a lesson. Or was it punishment? That kind of ass-whooping would not happen again, the staff assured us of that. It wouldn't be from lack of stamina, the way they ran us, that's for sure.

It was a normal Wednesday night. I had to rush to practice straight from working a 10-hour day like I normally did. Over a month deep into the season now and I was feeling great. I was back in my pre-surgery shape, and the extra time between games let the major bumps and sprains heal up a little easier.

We were having a quasi-scrimmage just to run starting defensive schemes and formations. I called the play, and we broke the huddle. I dropped back into coverage when Burnette dropped back to pass. I was all over it. He turned toward his running back in the flat and I jumped on it. I was well on my way to him before he'd even catch the pass.

I was approaching him fast and had started my breakdown, so I didn't overcommit to a certain direction. The running back cut left at the last second before I could slow down enough to square up. I stuck my right arm out in a desperate attempt to catch a handful of jersey to stop or at least slow him down. The next thing I felt was a sharp pain in my shoulder.

I was moving one direction and he was going fast in the opposite. My arm became the only thing caught in the middle of all that force and it felt like it was being torn off my body. I knew instantly that I was fucked. This was an all-new kind of pain. Sometimes your body just tells you, "I am done!"

I staggered to Coach Torregrossa and he had the trainer try and take my shoulder pads off. I winced in agony. The coach also knew I was done. He suggested that I go directly to the hospital and asked if I needed a ride.

I'd made it this far on my own, so I was going to leave the field on my own.

When I got in my car it took all of my manhood to not break down in tears. I already knew that my dream was over. I didn't need a doctor to confirm that.

I couldn't move my shoulder. It was frozen, as was my heart.

A torn subscapularis and torn labrum. That was the official diagnosis. In layman's terms, my shoulder was totally fucked up.

I would need surgery ASAP. I had to wait for all the swelling to go down, but the doctor wanted to get in there and repair the damage quickly and make sure there were no further hidden issues that the MRI didn't pick up.

Every man will go through a period of depression and self-doubt after a serious injury. It's how a man bounces back from those feelings that makes him a true man, a winner, a warrior.

I went through the woe-is-me moment for a spell. I asked God why after how hard I'd tried. Self-pity turned to frustration. Frustration transformed quickly to anger.

My emotions got the best of me for one day. That was all I allowed. Not even 24 hours. The second I pulled up to practice--and yes, I went back to practice the very next night--my whole outlook had changed. I found my heart again where I'd left it on the field the night before.

I wouldn't be the helpless victim ever again. I felt too much of that negative shit after my hernia surgery shutdown and I wouldn't let those emotions tackle my spirit ever again. I didn't have that anger anymore. I was completely resilient.

Morgan ran up to me first to examine my arm in a sling. I could tell he felt so badly. He knew my dream, and the fact that I'd finally lived it, however briefly. I might have even seen his eyes well up a little. He expressed how sorry he was, but at that moment it hit me. I had made it. I was talking to a teammate who cared about me on a professional football team that I'd played on at 30 years old, with zero football experience since my junior year in high school. I was part of something incredible: a family. Other teammates came up to check on me, and with every new face, I received more confirmation that I didn't need to be sad or mad. I was happy.

It was Thursday night, and the game was two days away.

I stayed at practice. I was part of this team and I wasn't about to leave them now. I could still contribute; maybe not on the field but from the sidelines: pumping them up, writing my Stinger newsletter, being the team photographer, and helping promote the club.

But even that was not enough for me. I missed the action. I needed more.

I showed up at the game walk-through practice on Friday night in full pads. My arm was still in a sling and hurt with every step. It may have slowed me down, but it wouldn't stop me.

Coach Torregrossa thought I was crazy to show up at practice ready to go, arm still in a sling. In the end, though, I was an adult, and he told me that if I wanted to risk further injury it was up to me.

I had no delusions; I knew that he wasn't going to allow me to participate in any contact drills. I suppose that I just wanted to make sure I was going to be a part of the team that I cared so much for, and still be allowed on the sidelines for the game. It would kill me to watch my brothers from the stands.

It was September 25, 1999, and I was the first one in the locker room before the game, as usual. Morgan arrived next as tradition had it, and I did my part to get him pumped up, although he didn't really need it.

When Torregrossa arrived, I pulled him aside and told him that I would be ready to go in an emergency situation if he needed me. He told me that he wasn't going to risk further damage to my shoulder by putting me in. I made him promise that he would keep an open mind and consider it. Okay, maybe I begged him. He agreed, but I

I think it was more to either humor me or shut me up. Regardless, I was active on the roster vs. the Georgia Panthers that day.

I was ready and antsy the whole game. I wanted nothing more than to get the call from coach to go in. I was ready to rip off my sling and go tackle everyone one-armed. It never happened. I never got the call. I didn't really expect to, but that didn't stop me from hoping.

We did not play well that day. I watched in pain from the sidelines, not because of my shoulder, but because I could not help my teammates and contribute in any significant kind of way.

It felt good to be in uniform, though I knew it would be my last time because surgery was inevitable now. I think I knew that deep down, so I had to make my comeback, however fruitless it was.

Our record of 2-2 was respectable on paper, but our only wins came from forfeits, which hurt. However, that wasn't the only way the Florida Stingrays were feeling a sting.

Not being able to play our first two games hit hard, and we never recovered from the loss of profit we'd expected from ticket, concession, and merch sales. Having to postpone the fourth game for financial reasons only set us back even further. By the time our next home game came around, the team was too far in the hole to continue. There was no operating money to rent fields or pay refs, let alone pay the players what they were owed.

The team had to fold and cease all operations. There was no way to go on, however hard we tried and with all the sacrifices we continued to make. It was very sad for the players, especially me. This Stingrays had become my entire life. I gave part of my life, and a limb, to them.

I don't blame them and harbored no ill will toward the franchise or owner. They did all they could, and I respect them for trying to keep it going as long as they did.

My professional football dream was already over due to injury, and now the entire team's was too.

In the end, I accomplished exactly what I set out to do. I fought through adversity, injuries, and age to become a 30-year-old professional football player with nothing more than two years of high school experience under my belt, armed with nothing but sheer will and determination. I beat overwhelming odds to manifest my own destiny and never, ever doubted myself or lost focus.

What many might consider as nothing extraordinary, I consider life changing. The entire experience from start to finish was a journey of self-discovery. I found confidence. I uncovered inner strength that I didn't know I possessed and may never have understood had I not endured what I did. I embraced passion and let it guide me through both physical and mental struggle. I revealed my resiliency and learned the power of absolute focus. Most importantly, I realized the truth in manifestation of destiny and in following my heart no matter what it wants or where it takes me.

All those personality traits and lessons born from my Stingray experience have stayed with me throughout life and only grown exponentially since. They guide me through life and have made me the strong, proud, and confident man that I am today. If there were no Florida Stingrays that man would not exist today.

I am so proud to say that I was a Stingray for a day.

EPILOGUE

Being a Stingray for that season satisfied my football career as a player and only grew my love for the sport exponentially. I've since had another shoulder surgery and my arthritic bad wing will be jacked up for life, but for every second of bad pain, I have a lifetime of good memories.

I moved back to Oregon a couple years after my Stingray season. I settled down and became a tattoo artist, actor and writer, but my unquenchable love for football always remained. I began coaching, with my neighbor and his kids, and discovered I loved that side of the game even more than playing.

Eventually I had a son of my own and he was destined to be a football fanatic from the start. I was very careful to not push Ryker too hard into the sport because I wanted nothing more than for him to find an unmanipulated and true love and passion for the game like I had so we could share a lifetime of bonding with the game.

I'll admit, reading stories of football legends to lure him to sleep and whispering tales of historic plays in his ear to stop him crying in his crib at night might have subtly swayed his outlook. He knew every team mascot by the time he was two, and he could say all the team names just from looking at their logos before he could say his ABC's.

He went straight into playing PeeWee tackle ball in kindergarten-his choice, and never looked back. I went straight into coaching his teams. We found a common passion that has forever bonded us by blood, sweat and tears through the years. We have fought together on the field and applied those lessons to his everyday life.

By third grade Ryker was starting quarterback and doing better than most QBs in the league. He was throwing touchdown passes while other kids were still fumbling snaps. I was now his head coach.

By sixth grade Ryker was playing tackle in the fall, flag in the winter and spring and doing QB camps in the summer, not to mention private quarterbacking lessons with the high school head coach Miles Haley every single week throughout the year. His dedication, sacrifice, and work ethic reminds me of my own journey with the Stingrays. He's already a better athlete than I ever was and has ran or thrown for well over 100 touchdowns, which is well over 100 more than I ever did.

I am teaching him to dream big and manifest his own destiny. I am still his head coach.

The happiness and satisfaction I got from football dream-come-true in 1999 fails in comparison to that which I get from watching my son play the sport. I was a Stingray for a day, but I am my son's #1 fan for life.

www.ingramcontent.com/pod-product-compliance
Lightning Source LLC
Chambersburg PA
CBHW062040290426
44109CB00026B/2687